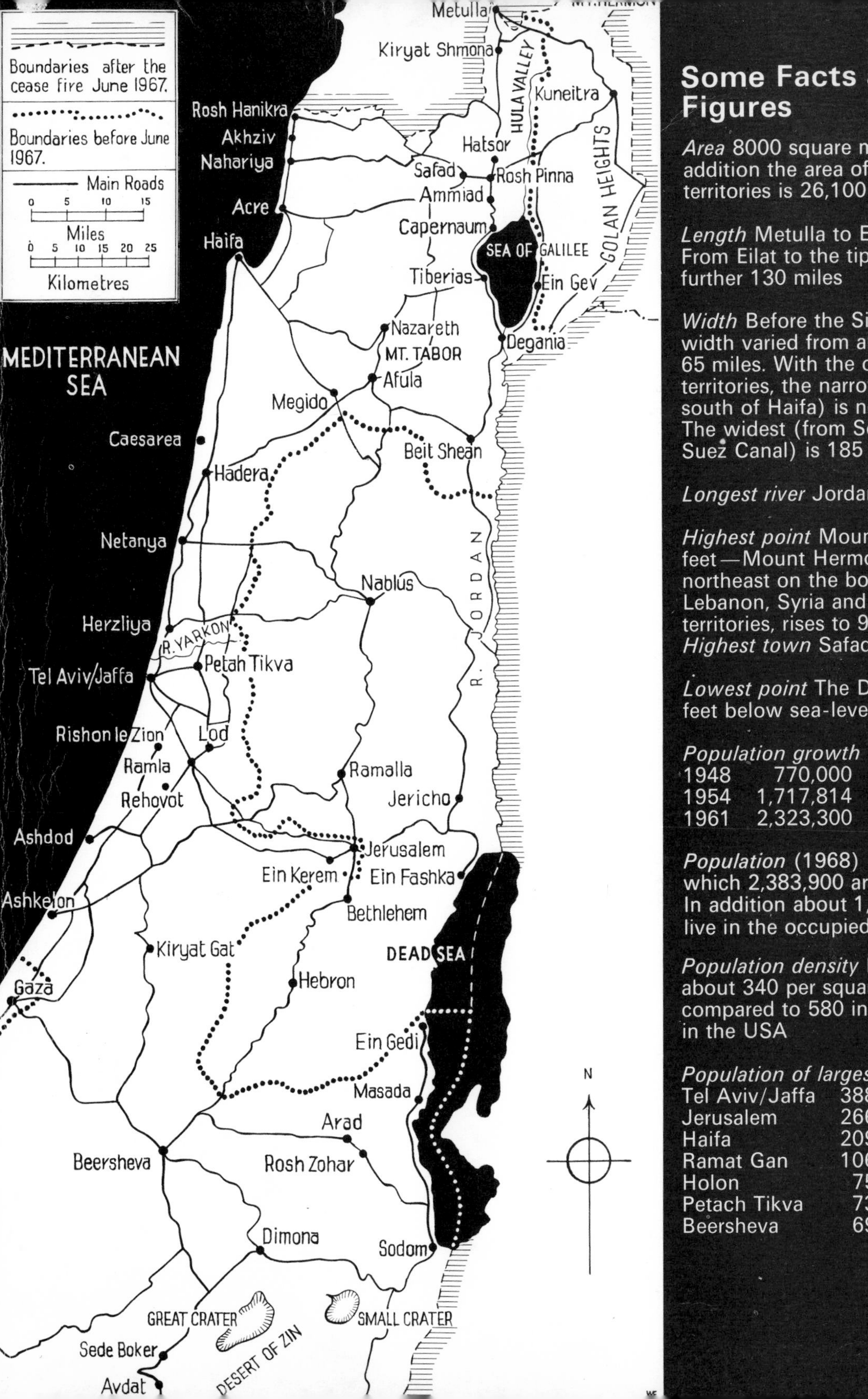

Some Facts and Figures

Area 8000 square miles. In addition the area of the occupied territories is 26,100 square miles

Length Metulla to Eilat 265 miles. From Eilat to the tip of Sinai is a further 130 miles

Width Before the Six-Day War the width varied from about 9 miles to 65 miles. With the occupied territories, the narrowest point (just south of Haifa) is nearly 40 miles. The widest (from Sodom to the Suez Canal) is 185 miles.

Longest river Jordan, 157 miles

Highest point Mount Meron, 3962 feet—Mount Hermon, in the northeast on the borders of Lebanon, Syria and the occupied territories, rises to 9000 feet.
Highest town Safad, 2790 feet

Lowest point The Dead Sea, 1290 feet below sea-level

Population growth

1948	770,000
1954	1,717,814
1961	2,323,300

Population (1968) 2,773,900, of which 2,383,900 are Jewish.
In addition about 1,000,000 people live in the occupied territories

Population density In Israel proper, about 340 per square mile, compared to 580 in Britain and 54 in the USA

Population of largest towns (1968)

Tel Aviv/Jaffa	388,000
Jerusalem	266,300
Haifa	209,900
Ramat Gan	106,800
Holon	75,900
Petach Tikva	73,500
Beersheva	69,500

Looking at ISRAEL

An Israeli soldier

Looking at

JONATHAN RUTLAND

Illustrated with 95 photographs by the author.

Adam and Charles Black London
J. B. Lippincott Company Philadelphia and New York

ISRAEL

Haifa Bay

Looking at Other Countries

Looking at HOLLAND

Looking at ITALY

Looking at NORWAY

Looking at GREECE

Looking at DENMARK

Looking at JAPAN

Looking at SPAIN

Looking at FRANCE

Looking at ISRAEL

Further titles in preparation

I should like to thank all the Israelis who helped me for their kindness and co-operation—in particular Clara and Moshe Grossman, Ida and Avri Adar, Avigail and Jack Katzenell; the members of kibbutz Ammiad and kibbutz Yotvata; and the staffs of the Israel Government Tourist Office both in London and Israel. I am also grateful to the Zim Israel Navigation Company for their assistance JR

All the photographs are by the author except for the one of Masada on page 62, for which acknowledgement is due to the Israel Government Tourist Office, and the one of the author on the back flap, which is by Lorna Rutland

The maps are by W. Fisher

SBN 7136 1040 9

FIRST PUBLISHED 1970

LIBRARY OF CONGRESS CATALOG CARD NUMBER: 75–104659
PRINTED IN GREAT BRITAIN BY *JARROLD & SONS LTD, NORWICH*

CONTENTS

The unit of currency in Israel is the Israeli pound, or lire, which is divided into 100 agorot. IL 1 (one Israeli pound) is worth about 2/5 (12 new pennies), or 29 cents.

Israel and the Israelis

The Judean Hills, near Bethlehem

Israel is one of the world's youngest countries, yet its history goes back 4000 years. It is one of the smallest countries, but one of the most energetic. It lies on the eastern shore of the Mediterranean Sea, at the cross-roads between Europe, Africa and Asia. For thousands of years the region has been a hub of life and activity, and of merchants trading and voyaging between Europe and the East. It was the land of the Jews and of their book, the Bible, and the home of Christianity. Nearly 2000 years ago the Jews were forced to leave their homeland, which became known as "Palestine". Today Jews from all over the world are returning to Israel to rebuild the country, a land of stony hills and hostile desert.

Down the middle of Israel, from north to south, stretches a backbone of mountains, not high peaks but the rounded hills of Samaria and Judea. Cutting across the mountains are several fertile valleys. The largest is the Jezreel Valley which runs from Haifa, the main port, to the River Jordan.

Palm Sunday procession in Jerusalem. Pilgrims from all over the world visit Israel, 'the Holy Land', to take part in festivals such as this

The Jordan is little more than a stream, but it is Israel's largest river and her main water-supply.

Jerusalem, the capital, stands in a commanding position on the Judean Hills, linked to Tel Aviv, Israel's largest city, by a belt of mountain villages. A few miles south of Jerusalem is Bethlehem, the birthplace of Jesus.

To the east the mountains drop steeply down to the Jordan and the Dead Sea, part of the Great Rift Valley which stretches from Turkey to Kenya. On the other side they slope gently down to the coastal plain. Most of the main towns are on or near the coast, including Tel Aviv.

In the south is the Negev Desert, dry and barren, but one of the most exciting parts of Israel both to look at and because of what the Israelis are doing with it. The landscape is ever changing, from the flattish Arava Valley which runs up from the Dead Sea to the Red Sea, to weird and fantastic-shaped mountains and giant volcanic craters.

The Ramon Crater in the Negev

Kiryat Shmona, a new immigrant town in the north

Modern Israel was founded in 1948 as a homeland for Jews, a place where they could be free to live as they liked. They poured in from over seventy countries. In 1948 there were about 650,000 Jews in Israel. During the first three and a half years an average of 500 immigrants arrived every day, so that by the end of 1951 the Jewish population had doubled.

The government bought battered old ships and aircraft to ferry immigrants. They sent a fleet of converted transport aircraft to carry 45,000 Jews from the Yemen on the Arabian peninsula. Many of them had never seen a car, let alone an aircraft, and they were frightened. But when Israelis told them they were going to fly to Israel they climbed aboard, believing that the Biblical prophecy was being fulfilled—that God would bring the Jews back to Israel "on eagles' wings".

Today tens of thousands of immigrants still arrive in Israel every year. There are about 12,000,000 Jews in the world, only 2,500,000 of them in Israel. Many will not immigrate to Israel because they are happy where they are (for example, those in Britain and America). Many others cannot come because their countries will not let them leave.

Israel had an enormous problem finding food, homes and jobs for the immigrants, especially since many of them had no money and knew no useful trade or work. New towns and villages were built in a hurry. At first people were sent wherever there was room, but later Israel's planners organized development areas such as the Lachish project, where a number

Young Israelis

of *moshavim* are grouped round a central town, Kiryat Gat. (A *moshav* is a co-operative village where each family has its own home and plot of land, but buying and selling are done co-operatively.) People in one moshav are all from the same country, so they live amongst familiar faces with familiar customs. When they visit Kiryat Gat, to shop or go to the cinema, they mix with people from other moshavim, and other countries. Gradually the different groups mingle, and become Israelis.

Some towns grew bit by bit, as people arrived. Others were planned down to the last detail before building began. Arad was established in 1962, in the middle of barren desert near the Dead Sea. Planners felt that the climate and central position in easy reach of Jerusalem, the Dead Sea and the Negev would make it popular with tourists. They studied raw materials to see what industries could be set up. They made detailed plans and building began. Today Arad is growing fast, and eventually 50,000 people will live there.

A school and homes in Arad

The Sea of Galilee near Tiberias

Israel has shores on four seas, the Mediterranean, the Red Sea, the Dead Sea, and the Sea of Galilee (the Dead Sea and the Sea of Galilee are both inland lakes). It also has hot and dry summers. From April until October rain is almost unheard of. So the beaches on all four seas are very popular. In midsummer the Mediterranean is busiest, as elsewhere it is too hot. In midwinter the Red and Dead Seas are still pleasantly warm. There is an entrance fee for many beaches, to pay for the facilities provided—shelters against the sun, drinking-water, showers, and lifeguards. Although the Mediterranean is almost tideless there are often dangerous undercurrents, and on many stretches of the shore swimming is forbidden. Everyone plays beach tennis, and Israeli men often do keep-fit exercises before going for a swim.

The northern half of the country sometimes gets a lot of rain in winter, but the most uncomfortable weather comes in spring and autumn with the *hamseens*, suffocatingly hot winds from the desert. The heat is oppressive, tempers are short,

Exercises on the beach

and there are more accidents on the road than at any other time of year—which is saying something as Israel has one of the world's worst records for traffic accidents. Israelis drive with a reckless lack of consideration for other people, overtaking on blind corners, pulling out in front of fast oncoming traffic, and generally making road travel nerve-wracking and dangerous.

This aggressive spirit is part of the Israeli character. In shops and restaurants it is no use waiting quietly to be served. Other people will often push in front of you. Perhaps this is all part of the fact that the country is still fighting for survival. Life is hard, working hours are long, and things are expensive. If you want to succeed you must push—hard.

There is a drive and sense of purpose about life in Israel. People know where they are going and are determined to get there. The goal is to make their country prosperous and peaceful, a safe and comfortable homeland for all Israeli citizens. Already they have come a long way since 1948. Israel is the most modern and industrial country in the Middle East.

Fruit is popular in the hot climate, and it grows well

Lizards like this are a common sight

People born in Israel are called *sabras*, after the *sabra* or prickly pear cactus which grows all over the country. Its fruit is covered with a mass of prickles, but inside it is soft and sweet. On the surface Israelis are hard and prickly. Yet few people are as generous and welcoming. Once you get to know them they will go out of their way to be helpful and kind. People say what they mean, and expect you to do the same. If you are offered a second piece of cake, do not say "no" politely and wait to be asked, "Are you sure?"

People are very informal. They usually dress casually. They do not hesitate to drop in on friends without an invitation and sit talking noisily and eating fruit and nuts for a couple of hours. The all-purpose greeting is *shalom*, peace. You use it when you meet someone, when you leave, when you go into a shop, and so on. Israelis do not bother with "please" (*b'vakasha*), but they do say "thank you" (*toda*). When someone gives you something you say *toda* and they say *b'vakasha* (which in this case means "you're welcome").

An outdoor café in Tel Aviv

A modern apartment in Jerusalem

Homes and Food

Homes are designed to keep out the heat and all that goes with it. They always have light stone-tiled floors which are cool, easy to clean and have no cracks or crevices to encourage insects. Most windows are fitted with a fine mesh wire screen to keep out mosquitoes and flies, and roller blinds to keep out the sun. Often there is a small balcony, a useful place to store things or hang washing. This too is built with some form of shuttering against the sun.

Israeli housewifes spend a lot of time cleaning. Every day they sweep their home thoroughly, wash the floors, shake the carpets, and air the sheets and blankets outside. At least once a week the house gets a spring-cleaning, which includes brushing or vacuuming the furniture and mattresses, and washing the woodwork. Up to a point all this is necessary, for in the hot dry climate sand and dust from outside gets everywhere, and ants, cockroaches and other insects can be a menace.

Most people live in compact one-floor apartments, made of concrete or stone. The main room is the living-dining room. Sabra families prefer simple modern furniture, while Yemenite Israelis like something exotic, with antique-style furniture, Oriental rugs, dried flowers, and many ornaments.

The kitchen is small, and its main piece of equipment is the refrigerator, large enough to serve as a general food store. Except for bread, potatoes, and canned and dried foods, everything is kept in it, including fruit, salad, jam and chocolate. Many housewives cook entirely on gas-rings or electric hot-plates, with no oven (Israelis do not roast meat).

To heat the home in winter there is a paraffin stove, and for hot water many houses have a solar energy water heater on the roof. The receptor is fixed at an angle to catch as much of the sun's heat as possible. Water in the pipes in the receptor rises as it gets hot, and flows into a storage tank. Two hours of sunlight is enough to provide a tankful of hot water, and for the days when the sun does not shine the tank is fitted with an electric heater.

Israeli cooking is a mixture of recipes from all over the world. People from Europe and America prepare traditional Jewish dishes such as gefilte fish (boiled fish-balls), and latkis (potato pancakes). Israelis from North Africa and the East have their own recipes, usually highly spiced.

Breakfast is early, especially in summer when work begins around seven. Most people have a cup of coffee or lemon tea and bread. But a proper breakfast consists of egg, cheese, pickled herring, salad, and yoghurt. The main meal is usually at midday. There is meat or fish, with rice, spaghetti or potatoes, followed by fresh fruit. Chicken is the most common meat.

A house with
a solar energy water heater

A local supermarket

The afternoon is siesta-time. Shops close at one o'clock and reopen from four to seven. Then in the evening people eat a light meal similar to breakfast, except on Friday—which is the big cooking day. The main meal of the week is on Friday evening, to welcome in the Sabbath (which runs from sunset on Friday to sunset on Saturday).

For fill-in snacks *felafels* are popular. Fried chick-pea balls, salad, pickles, and a spiced dressing are all crammed into a *pitta*—a flat Arab bread—and the result is delicious.

The Jewish religion has many rules about food. Milk products and meat must not be eaten at the same meal, and one must keep two sets of cooking-pots, dishes and so on, one for meat and the other for milk products. Pork is forbidden. Most restaurants follow these rules, so one cannot have coffee with milk or cream, or cheese, after meat. But at home only religious people follow the rules.

Artificial fish-ponds near Haifa—much of the fish eaten in Israel is bred in ponds like these

Arabs in Jerusalem

The Arabs

When the United Nations gave Israel independence in 1948 there were many Arabs living there. It had been their home for centuries. The Arab countries set out to destroy the new State of Israel, but they failed. Many Arabs fled—some lost their homes in the fighting, some did not want to live under the Israelis, and others left because the Arab governments told them to, promising them that Israel would be defeated.

Over 100,000 Arabs decided to stay in Israel. They became citizens of the new State, with the same rights as Jewish Israelis. They have their own towns, villages and schools, they keep their own religion (most of them are Moslems), they have their own Members of Parliament, and they share in the progress and prosperity of Israel.

But those who had fled, and the governments of the Arab countries, were still hostile and determined to retake Israel.

A mosque in Acre

Arab street vendors

They fired at villages near the borders and blew up roads and railways. They stopped Israeli ships from using the Red Sea and the Suez Canal, and they closed all the frontiers—so that it was, and still is, impossible to reach Israel except by sea or air.

Arab sabotage grew until at last Israel was forced to retaliate in the Sinai War of 1956. For a while the Arabs retired, but then again they started making terrorist attacks and again forced Israel to war, in 1967. In this Six-Day War Israel captured the Sinai Desert, East Jerusalem, the Golan Heights in the northeast, and the West Bank area of the Jordan Valley (including Jericho, one of the oldest cities in the world).

Israel still occupies these areas, with the great advantage that her borders are much easier to defend, and her ships can sail freely into the Red Sea and on to Africa and the East—but the problem of the 1,000,000 Arabs living in the occupied territories is unsolved. It may not be many years before Arabs outnumber Jews in Israel. They have larger families, and already they make up over a third of the population. Acts of sabotage within Israel are increasing and becoming more vicious—Arab terrorists plant bombs in supermarkets, cinemas and other public places. The Israelis make reprisal raids in an attempt to discourage the terrorists.

Nobody knows what will happen. Perhaps Israel will give back Sinai and the West Bank region, but only if peace is guaranteed. It is a difficult problem.

Jerusalem, the old city

Jerusalem

Jerusalem meanders from hill-top to hill-top on the crest of the Judean Hills. The setting is magnificent, and the city, sacred to Jews, Christians and Moslems, has a timeless atmosphere. There is an old Jewish saying that "God gave the world ten measures of beauty. Nine fell on Jerusalem and the other on the rest of the world."

Jerusalem is not the main shopping or commercial city of Israel. This makes it different from other capitals. There is no central area of luxury shops, cinemas and bright lights. The nearest approach is in and around the triangle made by Jaffa, Ben Yehuda and George V streets. Here the roads are always crowded and busy, but more like those of a market-town than a capital. The important places in Jerusalem are spread around the city.

Jaffa Street

Jerusalem means everything to Israelis, and to Jews all over the world. The most sacred place is the Western Wall, all that is left of the ancient Temple which was the hub of Jewish worship. Popularly called the "Wailing Wall", to look at it is nothing more than a large and very old wall made of immense stones. But for centuries Jews have made long and dangerous journeys to pray here. The Rabbis say that the spirit of God is always present at the Wailing Wall, and every day Jews gather here in prayer. There are many traditions associated with the Wall. One of the most popular is that of writing private prayers and slipping the note between the stones. Long ago, when Jews set out on a journey they would leave an iron nail between the cracks in the wall as a token of their attachment to their homeland.

The Wailing Wall

Scenes in Mea Shearim

One of the features of Jerusalem is the many men dressed in the traditional clothing of eastern European Jews—long black frock-coats and wide-brimmed velvet hats, and flowing beards and sidelocks. Most of them live in the city's religious quarter, Mea Shearim, a fascinating area of twisting alleyways and small courtyards, with prayer-houses, synagogues and religious training schools scattered everywhere. It has its own market and little workshops, and one can see traditional scribes at work.

The people of Mea Shearim observe Jewish Law down to its smallest details. Boys spend hours studying the Bible and religion from an early age, and wear sidelocks. On the Sabbath nobody does any work or cooking, nor will they travel in cars or light (or even switch on) a fire.

There is nothing old world about the Knesset, Israel's parliament, in the modern part of the city. Israel is a democracy, governed by the 120 members of the Knesset. Everyone over eighteen can vote in elections. One does not vote for a person but for a party, and each party receives seats in proportion to the number of votes it gets. This system is very fair but it makes for many political parties, so the government of the day is made up from a combination of several parties.

Across the road from the Knesset stands the Israel Museum. The most startling building is the Shrine of the Book where

TOP The Knesset from the Billy Rose Art Garden
MIDDLE The Shrine of the Book
FOOT Houses in the modern suburb of Gonen

the famous Dead Sea Scrolls are kept. The Scrolls were found in a cave beside the Dead Sea, and they contain Biblical and religious writings from about 100 B.C. The Samuel Bronfman Biblical and Archaeological Museum displays many interesting finds from prehistoric times, and the Billy Rose Art Garden, an open-air sculpture museum, is a popular spot with strollers. It overlooks a sports stadium and the modern buildings of the Hebrew University which, with over 10,000 students, is Israel's largest university.

On the hills around are some of Jerusalem's modern suburbs such as Kiryat Hayovel and Kiryat Menachem. Mostly the buildings are very plain, and their grey stone merges into the rocky hill-side. But in Gonen and a few other places the architects have been more adventurous.

LEFT Damascus Gate

RIGHT, TOP The Mosque of Omar
FOOT The Mount of Olives, with the Church of All Nations, the Garden of Gethsemane and the Russian church

The old city of Jerusalem is surrounded by splendid brown stone walls, built 400 years ago by the Turkish sultan Suleiman the Magnificent. Through the walls there are eight gates. Damascus Gate and Jaffa Gate mark the start of roads leading to those cities. The Lions' Gate is named after the lions carved in stone on each side, and the Dung Gate is so called because it was there that refuse was thrown out of the city. Beside Jaffa Gate the Citadel and Tower of David rise up from the city walls.

In the heart of the old city the Church of the Holy Sepulchre stands on the traditional site of the crucifixion, burial and resurrection of Jesus. Between the Lions' Gate and the church the Via Dolorosa marks the "way of the Cross", from where Pilate questioned Jesus to where he was crucified.

Near the church is the Christian quarter of old Jerusalem, with the Moslem quarter next to it, on the edge of the Temple Mount. The Jewish Temple was destroyed by the Romans nearly 2000 years ago, and today the site, known by Moslems as the "Noble Sanctuary", is crowned by two mosques. The largest is the Mosque of Aksa, with its silver dome. But the Mosque of Omar, a richly decorated octagonal building with a golden dome, dominates the scene. Inside there is a large rock which is believed by Jews to mark the spot where Abraham prepared to sacrifice Isaac, and by Moslems to mark the place from which Mohammed rose to heaven.

From the Temple Mount one looks across to the Valley of Kidron, the Mount of Olives and the Garden of Gethsemane.

Inside the old city

The Damascus Gate leads straight into the Oriental market, a crowded maze of covered alleys lined with Arab stalls and workshops, dark, mysterious and a little alarming. With the heavy smell of Arab foods and the general dirt, veiled women balancing loads on their heads, Arab men or boys leading over-loaded donkeys, crowds of people hurrying along—one feels in another world.

Coming out of the market the alleys are almost as narrow, but no longer covered, and most of the shops stock the work of Arab craftsmen—beautiful leather goods and beaten copper-ware, religious souvenirs and a mass of exotic oddments. This is a popular place both for Israelis looking for something to decorate their home, and for tourists. There are plenty of bargains to be had if one is prepared to haggle over the price.

In the old city, near the Holy Sepulchre

Dizengoff Circle

Tel Aviv/ Jaffa

In 1909 work began on Tel Aviv, the first new Jewish town to be built in 2000 years. The city has grown fast and now has over 500,000 people. There is a story that a politician, when asked the population, answered "Do you mean this morning or this evening?"

From the top of the Shalom Mayer Tower, the city's highest building, there is an impressive view of Tel Aviv, and of near-by towns such as Ramat Gan and Holon, which are all part of one sprawling mass of concrete buildings.

Tel Aviv is Israel's modern metropolis. The country's main museums, concert halls, cinemas and theatres are there, and almost every large Israeli firm has offices in Tel Aviv. In and around Allenby, the main street, are Israel's biggest and most luxurious shops. Allenby leads down to the sea front, where in the evenings crowds of people go for a stroll along the Herbert Samuel Esplanade. On one side there is a narrow strip of sandy beach, and on the other crowded cafés and the backs of tall office buildings. Dizengoff Street is also popular with people out for the evening, and its many pavement, or sidewalk, cafés are busy until late at night.

LEFT The Town Hall
RIGHT The Market

In 1909 the old town of Jaffa stood alone amongst the sand-dunes. Today Jaffa is still there, but it is little more than the old quarter of Tel Aviv. Many of the old houses have been pulled down, but near the shore dome-roofed houses, mosques and other buildings have been restored, and parks laid out round them. In one section artists have taken over, while in another Turkish bath houses have been turned into Oriental night-clubs and restaurants. The result is very picturesque, and provides a welcome contrast to the concrete of Tel Aviv.

Tel Aviv/Jaffa rises out of a belt of sand-dunes which stretch up the coast to Haifa and beyond, and down the coast to the desert. The dunes are gradually being built on or reclaimed. A few miles inland is Israel's international airport at Lod. To the north are the resort towns of Herzliya and Netanya; to the south the modern seaport of Ashdod, and Ashkelon where the weather is so reliable that hotels offer free rain insurance for visitors. And all around are orange groves—Jaffa oranges get their name from the old town of Jaffa.

A view of modern Tel Aviv from Jaffa. The tall building is the Shalom Mayer Tower

Haifa at dusk—nothing has gone wrong with the printing, it really does look like this (compare the frontispiece)

Haifa and Acre

The people of Haifa believe that their city is the most beautiful in Israel. It rises up the slopes of the Carmel Mountain, and from the top there are marvellous views of Haifa and the bay—a Middle Eastern rival to Naples, without the slums. The golden domed Bahai Temple, surrounded by Persian gardens, glistens in the sun, and the commercial area is spread out below.

At the foot lies Haifa port, with ships riding at anchor beyond. During the citrus-fruit season there are sometimes as many as twenty cargo boats waiting to come into the quays to load up with Jaffa oranges and grapefruit on their way to Europe. A pipeline leads from oil-refineries and storage tanks out to the bay, so oil-tankers do not need to dock at the busy quays.

Modern shops in the Carmel district of Haifa

Many visitors and immigrants arrive at Haifa, Israel's main port for passenger ships. Many travel on Zim liners. Zim, Israel's national maritime company, provide passenger and cargo services throughout the world, and her liners run popular cruises in the Mediterranean.

From near the port Israel's only underground railway, the Carmelit, travels up Mount Carmel, climbing 900 feet in a distance of just over one mile to Haifa's beautiful luxury suburb. From there a modern road runs along the crest of the Carmel range of hills, with a view up the coast to Lebanon and down to the Roman ruins of Caesarea and beyond. Inland the hills of Galilee are spread out like a map, with Mount Tabor clearly visible in the distance.

Haifa, Israel's third city, has its share of museums, its own symphony orchestra, and Israel's Institute of Technology—The Technion—where young people are trained as engineers, technologists and architects to play their part in developing their country.

North of Haifa the bay curves to Acre (Akko), one of the world's oldest seaports. There is an ancient tradition that glassmaking was discovered here, by fishermen who found that the heat of their fire had melted the silvery sand and made glass.

Acre

In the Middle Ages Acre was the main fortress and port of the Crusaders, thronging with merchants from Europe and the Orient. Today Haifa's port has taken over and the old port is used only by local fishermen. Around this is the old Arab quarter, a walled town with the remains of fortifications from Crusader times, and the domes and minarets of many mosques.

Old Acre has hardly changed for hundreds of years, but new Acre is a large modern town, full of recent immigrants and busy factories—including a "Steel City", separated from the rest by palm groves.

Beyond Acre the sand stretches north to the seaside resort of Nahariya, and on to Akhziv, once a Phoenician port but now a picturesque ruin deserted since the Arabs fled in 1948 (photograph page 63). A few miles further the road climbs up white cliffs to Rosh Hanikra, where the sea has carved grotto-like caves out of the rock.

And there the Lebanese border blocks the road. One can go no further.

Schools and Hebrew

Tzur Shalom school

Almost everything in Israel is expensive, so most mothers work to increase the family income. They can send their children to nursery school quite cheaply, and free education begins at the age of five, with a year at the kindergarten followed by elementary school from the ages of six to fourteen.

The photographs on these two pages show the elementary school at Tzur Shalom, a modern development suburb of Haifa. The normal school day in Israel is from eight o'clock until one, but here classes continue until three o'clock. The children go outside for ten minutes between lessons, and there are two half-hour breaks for meals—which the children help to prepare.

At the age of six children study reading, writing, mathematics, geography, history and natural science. Then in their second year they begin to study the Bible. To Israelis this is part of their history. They enjoy reading about the great men of the Bible, discussing the tactics of King Saul in his battles and King David's capture of Jerusalem. Naturally they read the Bible in its original language, Hebrew.

There are no organized games, but after school many children play basketball and soccer. One of the most popular "sports" in Israel is exploring. Some people go to a youth hostel such as the one at Ein Gedi where they are taken on walks in the area by members of the Nature Lovers Society. Others go off to the Negev in jeeps, with tents, food and plenty of water,

As part of their school day the children learn about animals and farming.

and spend several days exploring the desert, looking for caves, springs and unusual plants and rocks.

Pupils at Tzur Shalom's elementary school have plenty of opportunity for music and art and craft. Every boy makes a small sailing yacht in the woodwork-room, and the best boats take part in an annual race in Haifa Bay, with competitors from all over Israel.

Education is compulsory up to the age of fourteen, but many children go on to high school for a further three or four years' schooling. Then, when they are eighteen, they have to join up for their military service, which lasts two or three years. The armed forces play an important part in Israel. Everyone hopes that there will be peace between the Arab countries and Israel, but at the moment Israel must always be on the alert.

An art class

A modern school built on stilts—this helps to keep the rooms cool and provides a shaded playground

A signpost (Akko is Acre)

Children take learning foreign languages very seriously—Israel is the only Hebrew-speaking country in the world—and many Israelis can speak several languages. At the age of eleven children start learning English, and later many pupils study Arabic, the second official language in the country. As there are so many recent immigrants still struggling to learn Hebrew, and so many visitors who cannot speak or read Hebrew, road signs and notices in some shop-windows and restaurants are in English as well as Hebrew (and often Arabic). There are daily newspapers and broadcasts in several foreign languages, including English.

Many new immigrants from Europe and North Africa come to live in Tzur Shalom. When they arrive most of them cannot speak a word of Hebrew so the school runs special classes both for the children and their parents. After only four or five weeks the children have learned enough to start going to normal classes. But the parents find it more difficult and need to attend evening classes for several months before they can speak Hebrew at all fluently. So when their children come home in the evening they talk to their parents in their mother tongue.

Hebrew is quite unlike any European language. Sentences are made up differently, it is written from right to left, and no vowels are used. For beginners vowels are added in the form of dots and dashes, but before long pupils can recognize a word from its consonants and the vowels are left out. There are two alphabets, one for writing and one for printing.
The sentence below means "On Sunday we had dinner in the dining-room at school." It is first handwritten and then printed.

ביום ראשון אנחנו אכלנו ארוחת-צהרים
בחדר - האוכל של בית - הספר

ביום ראשון אנחנו אכלנו ארוחת-
צהרים בחדר האוכל של בית־הספר

The sentence is pronounced "Beyom rishon anachnoo achalnoo aruchat tzohorayim be hader ha-ochel shel beit hasefer." Translated word for word it means: "On day-first we ate meal-noon in room-the-food of house-the-book." (Days of the week are day-first to day-sixth and Sabbath. Many words such as *beit hasefer* are made up from combinations of words, so Hebrew has far fewer words than English.)

Older children see the younger ones across the road

The Kibbutz and Farming

General view of kibbutz Ammiad

There are not many ordinary villages in Israel. Most small settlements are either *moshavim* (co-operative villages), or *kibbutzim*. A *kibbutz* is a small farming village, but a village where nobody has any money, and where the main building is the communal dining-room. The word *kibbutz* is Hebrew for "group". Members of a kibbutz live together as a group, rather like a large family. They share the work, and in return receive everything they need. People choose to live on a kibbutz because they believe it is the best way of living.

Kibbutz Ammiad is in Upper Galilee, a few miles north of the Sea of Galilee. There are 114 members, plus their children—over 100 of them.

The dining-room is the hub of Ammiad. Everyone eats here, and after supper people sit about in groups chatting and making plans long after the meal is over. The works manager is there with his work chart for the next day, and the heads of the different departments tell him how many workers they need. The weekly movie film is shown in the dining-room, and on some evenings members join in folk-dancing or play badminton. At weddings and festivals everyone gathers here for the entertainments.

The photograph at the foot of the next page shows a meeting of the General Management Committee, which looks after the general running of the kibbutz. It discusses anything and everything—from, for example, whether to buy benches for the dining-room and whether to put a hard surface on the roads in the kibbutz, to examining the work of the different

The dining-room

departments. Often the Committee will decide something itself. But if the question being discussed means spending a large sum of money, or making any important change, it leaves the decision to the General Meeting.

The General Meeting is on Saturday evening. Every member takes part, and each person's vote counts equally. There are no bosses on the kibbutz—everyone is equal. The General Meeting controls the working of Ammiad. It elects the various officers (farm manager, secretary, treasurer, and so on) and committees. It discusses problems of all sorts, decides how money should be spent, and accepts new members—who come at first for a trial year, to see whether the kibbutz likes them, or they the kibbutz.

There are many other committees which help to run Ammiad, but they are all responsible to the General Meeting.

The General Management Committee

A married couple in their home

The private homes at Ammiad are like homes everywhere in Israel, but are smaller for members eat in the kibbutz dining-room, and children do not live in the same house as their parents. Newly married people have just one room, with a kitchenette and a shower. After five years or so they move into a larger apartment, with a second room which some keep for their children, and others use as a bedroom.

There is an allowance for furniture, and a list of "standard" items. But no two families use their allowance in the same way. One might decide on an expensive convertible couch, while another prefers to spend more on armchairs and less on the bed. Almost every home has a large and well-filled bookcase, and a good collection of classical records.

The houses are very comfortable, and Ammiad is a good place to live. But when the kibbutz was founded in 1946 there was nothing here except rough stony land and one or two trees. The kibbutz was positioned at Ammiad to settle the land and to protect the Tiberias–Rosh Pinna road against Arab attack. The thirty founder-members lived in tents for the first few years, and they had to collect all their water from Rosh Pinna, five miles up the road. Life was difficult and primitive, and the members often wondered whether it was worth carrying on. But at last in 1950 a water-pipe was laid, and since then the kibbutz has grown steadily.

In 1951 twenty people arrived from Jewish youth movements in Holland. Then followed sixty from Britain, and some small groups from youth movements in Israel; and more people are arriving every year. Many discover that they do not like kibbutz life. They prefer to be independent, so they leave and find jobs in town.

The photograph on this page shows Ammiad's general shop. Everyone gets an annual allowance for use in this shop, and another for use in the clothes store. When a member "buys" something the cost is marked on his card so that he always knows how much he has spent—but no money is used.

There is a separate annual "holiday allowance" of IL 210 which most people spend on books, record players, cameras and other luxuries. For their holidays they go for a few days to Ammiad's seaside house, and to the kibbutz's apartment in Tel Aviv.

The kibbutz shop

One of the children's playrooms

The children have their own village in the middle of the kibbutz. Six children live in each house, and they have their own club-rooms, dining-rooms, and a kindergarten and school.

The children get up at seven o'clock, fitting in a lesson before breakfast. There are more lessons until lunch at midday. Older children have classes after lunch, and then later in the afternoon they work on their farm. They keep goats and chickens and a small market garden. The goats' milk is made into cottage cheese which is popular in the dining-room. All the produce from the children's farm goes to Ammiad's kitchen.

After the day's work children go to their parents' houses for the afternoon, and they are with them all day on the Sabbath.

Instead of organized games there are regular outings and hikes, and the children make good use of the kibbutz's basketball court. They start learning to swim when they are three years old, and in the summer they use the swimming-pool every day.

There is always more than enough work, so the mothers work a full six-day week, and the children help more and more around the kibbutz as they get older. At the age of eighteen they have to go into the army, where they get their first experience of life outside the kibbutz. Most of them decide to return afterwards to become full working members.

Part of the beef herd in the portable corral

Ammiad grows all sorts of fruits and keeps a beef herd, dairy cows and chickens. The beef cattle live out on the ranch, ranging over an enormous area of natural pastureland. The land is too rough for vehicles so the herd is looked after by two men on horseback. They have a portable corral which is set up on the ranch when the cattle need spraying against disease.

Citrus fruits are one of Israel's most important crops, and citrus groves are a familiar sight all over the northern half of the country. The best of the fruit is exported under the Israeli trade name "Jaffa". At Ammiad the fruit is picked into buckets and transferred to large wooden crates which are pushed to the end of the row of trees along movable railway lines. The railway lines are constructed in Ammiad's factory, which produces all sorts of light farm machinery. Originally the kibbutzim were strictly farming settlements, but today many have factories, producing anything from toys to luxury furniture.

Picking oranges

Trimming and clearing in the banana plantation. On the right there is a bunch of fruit wrapped in paper

Ammiad's banana plantations are beside the Sea of Galilee in the Upper Jordan Valley. The soil there is better for bananas than the heavier earth up on the actual kibbutz, and the climate is hotter and more moist. Also bananas need more water than any other crop in Israel, if not in the world, and pumps beside the Sea of Galilee provide a plentiful supply.

Israel is not a natural banana-growing country. Bananas grow best in tropical countries like Jamaica, where the weather is much the same all the year. The Jordan Valley has a sub-tropical climate—the winter can be cold, between mid-February and mid-March temperatures rocket up from 57 °F to 95 or 105 °F, and the summers are dry and very hot. Even so bananas are grown successfully in the Jordan Valley.

A great deal of time must be spent protecting the bananas from the weather. In winter each bunch of fruit is wrapped in brown paper to keep out the cold, and in August they are again wrapped to prevent the almost ripe bananas from being blackened by the scorching sun.

Carrying a "head" of fruit to the end of the row for collection

Picking avocado pears. The picking platform was made in Ammiad's factory

The plantations were originally irrigated by flooding the ground, but Ammiad is installing new sprinkler irrigation which, although expensive to set up, is much cheaper to run. The sprinklers are placed near the base of the plant. (If the foliage gets wet it quickly becomes sunburned.)

The fruit is harvested throughout the year. Each bunch is wrapped in sacking, loaded on to a trailer and taken to a central packing station where the best fruit is selected and sent to Haifa for export. The rest is sold in Israel.

Avocado pears grow well and they sell for a good price. Once ready for picking the fruit can be left on the trees for up to three months without becoming spoiled. When an order comes in enough fruit is picked to fill the order and the rest is left on the tree. The fruit hangs inside the tree, where it is protected from the sun, but is awkward to pick.

Olives, peaches and pecan nuts all give good harvests, but the apple and pear orchards have so far been less successful. The trees have a short working life of only ten years. This is probably because there is so little cold weather—orchards in the same region but higher up the hills do much better. Ammiad is trying out special trees which are trained in a fan shape along wires. They should produce more fruit, which will help to offset the short working life.

All the orchards have to be irrigated during the dry months from March to October.

The River Jordan

The Waters of Galilee

Most of Israel's land is in the southern part of the country, and is desert. Most of the water is in the north—the Galilee region is the wettest part of Israel, and the Sea of Galilee provides the country with a huge natural reservoir. At the top of the lake, not far from where the River Jordan enters, there is an underground pumping station which sends the water on its way along a large pipeline to Tel Aviv, where it joins water from the River Yarkon, and on to desert towns such as Beersheva and Arad. There it is piped to houses and to the fields for irrigation.

Because water is scarce in Israel it is valuable. No expense is spared in making sure that it is put to the best use. On the shores of the Sea of Galilee there is a laboratory which keeps a constant check on the water of the lake, and works on ways of improving its quality by, for example, trying to keep down microscopic animal life. It is also vital to keep the water as "sweet" as possible. The Sea of Galilee is over 600 feet below sea-level, so many of the springs which feed the lake are salty. Some of these springs come from the bed of the lake, and nothing can be done about them beyond observing their effect, and notifying the mixing stations down the line when the water is particularly salty. But others reach the lake as streams, and they are diverted and go on down to the Dead Sea, where the salt is put to good use.

Beside the Sea of Galilee

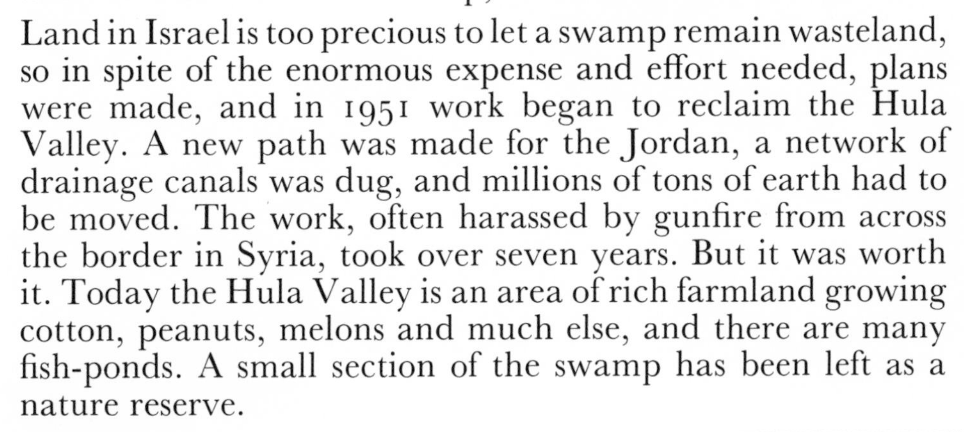

North of the Sea of Galilee, there are plenty of sweet water springs, but even here the water is very expensive. The region is so hilly that to get water to many of the settlements it has to be pumped up as high as 2000 feet. Most of the springs are in the Hula Valley, which not so long ago was a swamp. Millions of years ago erupting volcanoes poured their lava into the path of the River Jordan. The river was forced to leave its normal course, and the area became a swamp, useless and disease-ridden.

Land in Israel is too precious to let a swamp remain wasteland, so in spite of the enormous expense and effort needed, plans were made, and in 1951 work began to reclaim the Hula Valley. A new path was made for the Jordan, a network of drainage canals was dug, and millions of tons of earth had to be moved. The work, often harassed by gunfire from across the border in Syria, took over seven years. But it was worth it. Today the Hula Valley is an area of rich farmland growing cotton, peanuts, melons and much else, and there are many fish-ponds. A small section of the swamp has been left as a nature reserve.

The Hula Valley with Mount Hermon in the distance

In Safad's artists' quarter

Safad, Tiberias and Nazareth

From Safad (pronounced Tsfat), perched high on a mountain-peak, one can see south to Mount Tabor and the Sea of Galilee, east across to the Golan Heights, and north to the Lebanon. Safad is Israel's highest town and near by is one of the highest peaks, Mount Meron. With its magnificent scenery, and the clean air, the town is popular with holiday-makers and with artists—the old Arab quarter is now a busy artists' colony.

Tiberias, the main town on the Sea of Galilee, was named after the Roman emperor Tiberius. In early times the Romans came here to bathe in the hot springs, which are still one of the attractions of the town.

Tiberias, 670 feet below sea-level, is one of the world's lowest cities, which accounts for its hot climate. It is a popular resort, with bathing beaches, water-skiing, and boat trips on the lake—across to kibbutz Ein Gev, which holds an annual music festival; south to Degania, the first kibbutz; and north to Capernaum, where Jesus preached.

A café in Tiberias

A street market in Nazareth

Above Capernaum rises the Mount of Beatitudes, the traditional site of the Sermon on the Mount. All over the Galilee there are places mentioned in the Bible—Mount Gilboa, where David mourned the death of Saul and Jonathan ("How are the mighty Fallen"); Mount Tabor, where Deborah won her victory over the Canaanites; and Nazareth, the town where Jesus spent his childhood.

According to the New Testament it was in Nazareth that the Angel Gabriel appeared to Mary to announce the coming birth of Jesus, and over the Holy Grotto an enormous Church of the Annunciation has been built. The town is bristling with churches and hostels, and the shops are full of souvenirs, ranging from crucifixes to small jars of "Nazareth soil".

The people of Nazareth are mostly Arabs, and it is a typical Arab town, full of old houses, steep and winding alleys, small shops and busy markets. Near by is Upper Nazareth, a modern Jewish town providing homes and work for immigrants, and a balance to the non-Jewish old town.

The Church of the Annunciation

Jewish weddings are held under a canopy. This kibbutz wedding is in a small oasis in the desert—the canopy is held up with pitch-forks and rifles to symbolize the kibbutz's aims of farming and defending the land

Religion and Festivals

The Jewish religion is based on the first five books of the Bible (the Torah, or Law), and the teachings of the Rabbis who explain the Law and give precise instructions about everyday life. About fifteen percent of Jewish Israelis keep the laws strictly, and nearly thirty percent go to synagogue every week.

The Jewish New Year falls in September or October,* and on the tenth day is the Day of Atonement. For religious people this is the most solemn day of the year, a day of fasting and prayer. Succot, the Feast of Tabernacles, begins a few days later and lasts one week. During this festival each family builds a small roofless hut, covered with greenery and decorated with flowers. They eat their meals in this "tabernacle". Succot is a reminder of the forty years the children of Israel wandered in the wilderness living in temporary homes.

Next comes Hanuka, the Feast of Lights, in memory of Judas Maccabaeus' victory over the Greeks, who tried to force the Jews to worship Greek gods. On each of the eight days of Hanuka a fresh candle is added to the eight-branched Hanuka candelabrum. Every family has a candelabrum at home, and all over the country public buildings have large electric ones on the rooftop. Hanuka comes near the Christian Christmas, and like Christmas it is a time for giving presents.

* 13 September 1969 to 1 October 1970 was the year 5730 in the Jewish calendar.

Late in January is the New Year of the Trees, when children plant thousands of saplings on the hill-sides and join in songs and dances. Then at Purim, early in March, children dress up in fancy costume to celebrate the time when Esther rescued the Jews in Babylon. The story is told in the Book of Esther in the Bible.

The other important religious festival is Passover, which commemorates the escape of the Jews from slavery in Egypt, and their return to Israel—the Exodus. On the eve of the first day, families gather around the table to read and sing the Exodus story, and to eat a special Passover meal. There are bitter herbs as a reminder of the bitter years of slavery, and instead of bread one eats matzos, an unleavened bread, in memory of the original Passover when the fleeing Jews had no time to make proper bread. Throughout the week-long festival there is no bread in the shops, just giant boxes of matzos.

Two weeks after Passover, Independence Day is celebrated with enthusiastic festivities, fireworks and dancing in the streets.

TOP The Festival of Purim

RIGHT Religious men in Jerusalem

The Dead Sea near Sodom—one of the large dikes can be seen in the middle of the photograph

The Dead Sea

From Arad the road drops steeply from the Judean Hills, through weird and desolate lunar-like landscapes and stifling heat to the lowest place on earth, the Dead Sea. Southwards lie the sites of the ancient cities of Sodom and Gomorrah, but no signs of either of them exist now—just a mass of contorted cliffs and pillars of salt. To the north the road passes Masada and leads to Ein Gedi, an oasis of green with freshwater springs feeding a waterfall and a beautiful natural swimming-pool. There is a kibbutz, a youth hostel and camping site, and a nature reserve with fragrant balsam trees and wild gazelle. The mountains around are honeycombed with caves, and it was not far north of Ein Gedi that the Dead Sea Scrolls were found.

The River Jordan flows into the northern end of the Dead Sea, but as it is the lowest place on earth no water can flow out again. It is also one of the hottest places in the world, which means that the water does eventually escape, by evaporation. This process has been going on for millions of years. All the minerals which the Jordan and other streams bring to the Dead Sea have collected there, and it is now eight times as salty as ordinary sea-water. Every pint contains a quarter of a pound of salt.

Nothing can live in water as salty as this, and non-swimmers

Kibbutz Ein Gedi

can swim safely. The sea is so buoyant that one floats half out of the water, with no effort. It is impossible to sink, and difficult to swim as arms and legs tend to ride up on top of the water. But lying back and relaxing in the silky water is a novel experience, and the Dead Sea and the sulphurous springs which flow into it are good for skin diseases and rheumatism.

Far more important, the Dead Sea is Israel's largest single source of mineral wealth, which is exploited by the Dead Sea Works at Sodom. Water is enclosed in large ponds, and when it has evaporated it leaves behind a layer of salt topped by a thinner layer of potash. At first this was done on a fairly small scale, but now, with the help of Dutch and American engineers, dikes have been built enclosing the southwestern part of the Dead Sea, to make an evaporation pan of nearly forty square miles.

Once collected, the minerals are refined and processed and sold all over the world for use by farmers, chemists and industry.

Beside the Dead Sea—to the left is the Dead Sea itself, and to the right are freshwater pools where one can wash off the salty water

The Desert of Zin

The Negev Desert

Once every few years, after a particularly wet winter, the desert turns green for a few weeks. But normally the Negev is about as barren and desolate as one could imagine. A scattering of low burned-looking grey-green trees and small shrubs somehow manage to keep alive, but that is all. It looks useless, and for a long time most experts said it was useless. Rain hardly ever falls, in summer the sun is blisteringly hot, and in winter the temperature sometimes falls below freezing at night. Most of the water in the area is salty.

But Israelis do not seem to know the word "impossible", and those who had studied their Bible knew that in Biblical times many people had lived and farmed in the Negev. In any case Israel is a small country, over half desert, and homes, food, and jobs had to be found for the new immigrants pouring in—perhaps the desert could provide all of these. So work began with geologists searching for minerals, groups of adventurous people starting small farming settlements, and archaeologists studying ancient methods of farming.

Forty miles south of Beersheva, dominating the desert from its

Avdat

mountain-top position, stands the ruined city of Avdat. It was built by the Nabataeans (who came from Arabia), probably in the first century B.C. The city was on a cross-roads of routes across the Negev, and the people of Avdat earned their livelihood providing food and shelter to caravans and armies passing through the area. The desert around looks absolutely barren. It is the Desert of Zin, where Moses and the children of Israel almost died of thirst. But the Nabataeans learned to collect such rainfall as there was in underground cisterns. They collected the water over a large area, and used it to irrigate a small area of farmland. Today scientists are studying and re-creating their methods, and have succeeded in growing crops in the desert at Avdat. Thus irrigation methods 2000 years old are helping to bring life back to the Negev today.

Of all the regions of the Negev, the one condemned most as unfit for anything was the Arava Valley, running along the border with Jordan. But even in this remote and desolate region settlements were founded, one of them kibbutz Yotvata, near Eilat.

Beduin caravan near Beersheva

An experimental plot, growing peppers under plastic. The fences are wind-breaks

Yotvata

Yotvata began in 1951 as a border garrison, manned by eighty young men and women who had decided to leave the security and comfort of life in the towns to do pioneering work in the desert. They pitched their tents, built a pumping station to get water from underground, and set to work clearing "fields" in the sand, rigging up irrigation pipes and sprinklers, and putting up houses. They tried growing everything, and although many crops failed they were successful with dates and tomatoes. They tried keeping sheep, and when that failed they bought a few dairy cows.

Today Yotvata is a thriving agricultural settlement, a startling patch of green in the desert, with a herd of 120 dairy cows and over 10,000 chickens, supplying Eilat with all the milk and eggs the town needs. They have a large date plantation, and specialize in growing summer vegetables in winter, which is very profitable. They have their own laboratory experimenting on what can be grown in the desert, and how best to grow it. The dairy herd is one of the wonders of Israeli farming. Few people had thought one could raise cattle in the desert, with no pastureland and with such hot summers. The cattle live in open sheds, all their food is brought to them, they get three showers a day in summer; and they are one of the finest herds in the country.

The cattle pens and sheds

Money earned from the produce has been used to modernize the kibbutz. The members now have very comfortable homes set amongst trees and lawns. Every home has its "desert cooler", a device with an electric fan blowing air through layers of damp mattress-like material; and the buildings are designed to keep out the heat. Even so life in the desert can be difficult and uncomfortable. In summer work begins at four o'clock in the morning, since the heat makes it impossible to do anything but sleep in the afternoon. Occasional sandstorms create chaos. The sand gets into everything. And the rain when it comes, is so heavy that the sand cannot soak it up fast enough.

From the start one of the kibbutz's major problems was water. There are good supplies of underground water in the Arava, but it, like the desert sand, is very salty. At last even this problem seems to have been solved, by an experimental device which removes the salt from the water by reverse osmosis. The machine consists of two pumps and nearly 500 yards of metal tubing, lined with a special skin. Under pressure from the pumps, sweet water passes through the skin, leaving the salt behind. So soon, for the first time, the kibbutzniks will have sweet water to drink.

The desalination plant

Mitzpe Ramon

Industry, Beersheva and Beduins

While settlements like Yotvata were showing that the desert could be made to bloom, geologists were successful in their search for minerals in the Negev. Oil was struck near Ashkelon, and gas at Rosh Zohar near the Dead Sea. Large deposits of phosphate rock found around the Great Crater are used for making chemical fertilizers. The copper-mines at Timna, originally worked during the time of King Solomon, were reopened after a break of 3000 years. Flint clay for ceramic ware is mined at Mitzpe Ramon, there is glass sand at Eilat; and much else. The underground wealth of the Negev is greater than anyone had hoped.

To exploit all these raw materials new roads and railways were built, along with new towns and factories; and somehow people had to be encouraged to settle and work in the desert. Many young people settle in the Negev because they enjoy the excitement and challenge of pioneering work. But others want comfortable houses, good shops and cinemas, before they are willing to live and work in the desert. So new towns such as Dimona have been built, and the capital of the Negev, Beersheva, has grown from a handful of inhabitants in 1949 to a modern town bursting at the seams with almost 70,000 people.

Kibbutz Yotvata. Beyond the houses are the fields,
and beyond them the frontier and the mountains of Edom in Jordan

Modern blocks of apartments in Beersheva

As more and more people have come to Beersheva—and they come from over fifty different countries—new suburbs have been built for them. Each district has its own schools, shops, synagogues and so on. The town has spread out over the desert, with groups of houses and apartments all over the place, areas of sandy wasteland, and constant building of yet more homes and factories.

Scientists from all over the world come to Beersheva's Negev Institute for Arid Zone Research to help in the struggle to bring life to the desert. They experiment with a wide variety of plants and trees to see if they can be successfully adapted to the conditions of the Negev, and they try out different ways of growing them. One method is called "hydroponics"—plants are grown in gravel, and water with the exact amount of chemicals needed by the particular plant is circulated through the gravel beds. This method uses less water than straightforward irrigation. It is expensive to build the gravel beds, but once set up, hydroponics provides a successful way of growing out-of-season vegetables and flowers in the desert.

Other experiments set out to harness the energy of the sun, to convert salty water into sweet water, and to discover the effects on people of desert life.

Growing sisal in the desert—an experimental crop

The Beduin market, Beersheva

From modern factories and research to Beduin shepherds living much as they have lived since Biblical times, leading their camels and herds of sheep and goats across the desert in search of pasture—this is one of the contrasts of Beersheva. The long black Beduin tents are a familiar sight around the town. Early every Thursday morning the Beduins hold their market in Beersheva, bartering amongst themselves for anything from vegetables to camels and tractors, and selling traditional copperware, camel-packs and hand-woven rugs to tourists.

More and more the Beduins are beginning to settle down, to buy tractors and trucks, and to live in shanty towns of tin huts (which must get unbearably hot in the summer, unlike their traditional goatskin tents which keep out the heat). Some Beduins have left the desert altogether to live in modern villages near Beersheva. Many others still live in their tents, but go to work in factories and on building sites in Beersheva and Arad—which explains bus stops by the roadside mysteriously placed in the middle of apparently empty desert.

Eilat

Eilat, with the airport in the foreground

At the southern tip of the Negev lies the frontier town, port and winter holiday resort of Eilat. In 1949, when Israeli settlers arrived, there was just one deserted hut, but today Eilat is one of Israel's most important new towns. Standing at the head of the Gulf of Aqaba, just across the border from the Jordanian port of Aqaba, it provides a vital outlet via the Red Sea to East Africa, India and the Far East—vital because the Egyptians refuse to allow Israel's ships to pass through the Suez Canal.

Heavy trucks travel down to Eilat carrying copper from Timna, chemicals from the Dead Sea industries, bathroom fittings from Beersheva—all for export from Eilat's rapidly growing port. The trucks return to northern Israel carrying enormous tree-trunks from Africa and goods imported from the Orient.

Eilat has a small airport linking it with the north, and an oil pipeline to Haifa port.

More and more people are going to Eilat for a winter holiday. The climate is ideal, and the reddish mountains on either side of the gulf, reflected in the brilliant blue of the sea, make a beautiful setting—with unbelievable sunsets when the mountains turn to shades of deep red and purple. Even in mid-January, the sea is warm and the temperature just right for sunbathing. At night it rarely falls below 50 °F and during the day 75 °F is normal; rain is almost unheard of, and Eilat claims almost 365 sunny days a year. One can hire flippers, face-mask and snorkel, and spend hours looking through the crystal-clear water at the tropical fish swimming among underwater ferns and coral reefs. Alternatively one can go for a cruise in a glass-bottomed boat.

Eilat is booming. Already nearly 15,000 people live there. Yet despite the shortage of water there are plans for expanding it to four times its present size. The only possible source of water is the sea, and an experimental desalination plant is in action, providing thirty percent of the town's water. The process is expensive, but scientists are continually experimenting, and less costly methods may be found—in fact they must be found if Eilat is to grow as planned, and the Negev Desert be developed to the full.

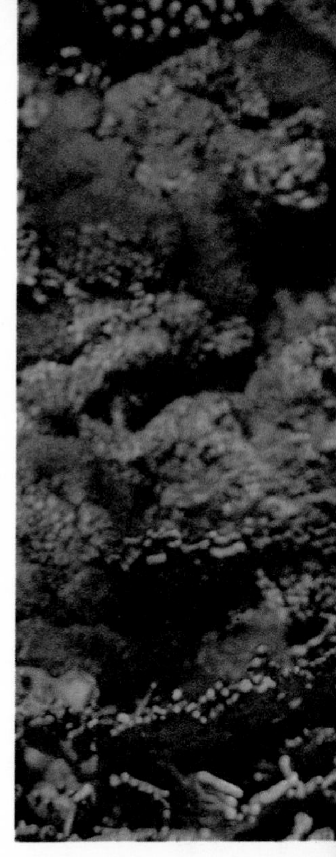

Corals, seen from a glass-bottomed boat

The beach at Eilat, with the mountains of Sinai in the background, photographed in mid-January

Part of a model of Jerusalem at the time of the Second Temple. The Temple is in the foreground

4000 Years of History

Nearly 4000 years ago Abraham moved from his home near the River Euphrates and journeyed south to Canaan. The Bible describes how God revealed to him that this land would belong to him and his descendants. Abraham and his people were called "Hebrews" until, in another revelation, Abraham's grandson Jacob was renamed Israel ("the champion of God"). His descendants were "the children of Israel" (later to be called "Jews"), and Canaan became the land of Israel.

During a time of drought and famine the children of Israel sought refuge in Egypt, where they were later forced into slavery. Moses led the exodus back across the Red Sea and Sinai to Israel. The Bible relates how, at Sinai, God gave Moses the Ten Commandments and the Torah (the Law). The "children of Israel" became "the people of the book".

Around 1000 B.C. King David united the various kingdoms of Israel, and made Jerusalem the capital of his kingdom. His son Solomon built a splendid temple there, and during his reign Israel was peaceful and prosperous.

Peace did not last. About 586 B.C. Jerusalem was destroyed by Nebuchadnezzar, and its inhabitants taken captive to Babylon. About fifty years later they were allowed to return and build a Second Temple.

In 168 B.C. Antiochus Epiphanes, King of Syria, captured Jerusalem and destroyed the Second Temple. The Jews fought

Part of Herod's Palace, Masada

their invaders fiercely, but in 65 B.C. they were faced by the massive forces of the Roman Empire and the odds against them were too great.

About 37 B.C. the Romans appointed Herod the Great to govern as King of Judea. Herod built many public buildings, including a new Temple, as well as luxurious palaces and fortresses. The Temple of Herod re-established Jerusalem as the hub of worship for the Jewish religion.

After Herod's death in 4 B.C. there were numerous uprisings against Roman rule, and finally in A.D. 70 Rome sent in an army to conquer the rebels. Jerusalem was destroyed, and with it all but the Western Wall of the Temple.

On a mountain-top beside the Dead Sea, a determined group of 1000 men, women and children held out against the besieging Romans for three years. Their stronghold was the sumptuous fortress-palace of Masada, built by King Herod. When it was obvious they could hold out no longer, the Jews voted to commit mass-suicide rather than surrender. To the Israelis today, Masada stands as a symbol of heroism in the fight for freedom.

Unwilling to live under Roman rule, many Jews fled into exile, and during later invasions—by Arabs, Crusaders, and Turks, among others—many more were forced to leave their land.

Some Israeli stamps

The menorah
(seven-branched candelabrum)
the symbol of modern Israel—
which stands near the Knesset

The Israeli flag

For the next 2000 years the Jewish people were dispersed throughout the world. Wherever they lived they kept their religious traditions. Because their religion differed from that of the people of their new homelands, Jews were always somewhat set apart. In many countries these differences led to persecution and hardship.

Every year at Passover Jews have prayed "next year in Jerusalem", believing that someday they as a people would return to Israel. Throughout the centuries a few did manage to go back. At the end of the nineteenth century, when persecution of Jews in Russia was severe, many fled to Israel.

They found that the great forests described in the Bible had been cut long ago, and soil had eroded leaving barren and stony ground. Lowland areas, which had been rich farmland, were swamps infested with malarial mosquitoes. Undaunted, they bought land and set to work to reclaim it. Their example encouraged thousands more, as did the efforts of Theodor Herzl who, in 1897, founded the World Zionist Organization; its aim was to create a national home for the Jewish people.

In 1917 the British Government announced its support of Zionism, and in 1922 the League of Nations followed suit, entrusting the government of Palestine to the British. Jews streamed into Palestine, setting up farms and factories, towns and villages. By 1939 Palestine was in chaos. The Arab leaders had turned violently anti-Jewish; and the British, anxious not to offend the Arabs, tried to stop Jewish immigrants from entering. The Jews resisted both the Arab violence and the British restrictions.

Akhziv—once a busy Arab town, it has been deserted since the War of Independence in 1948

Hitler's rise to power in 1933 had given a new urgency to the plight of the Jews. By the end of World War II, Hitler and his Nazis had exterminated 6,000,000 Jews, and left behind thousands of refugees who had somehow survived the horrors of the concentration camps.

In 1947 the United Nations Organization finally agreed, despite Arab hostility, to give the Jews a national home. On 14 May 1948 Israel became an independent State, and for the first time in nearly 2000 years the Jews had a homeland. But the fight was not over. As the British pulled out, the seven Arab nations (with a total population of 35,000,000) invaded, determined to kill the new State of Israel at birth. The Jews (only 600,000 of them), with the Nazi horror fresh in their minds, were prepared to suffer any hardship to win their homeland, and to be able to live in peace. Watched by an astonished world, the Israeli soldiers defeated the Arabs on every side. The miracle had happened, and Israel opened its doors to Jews from all over the world.

Index

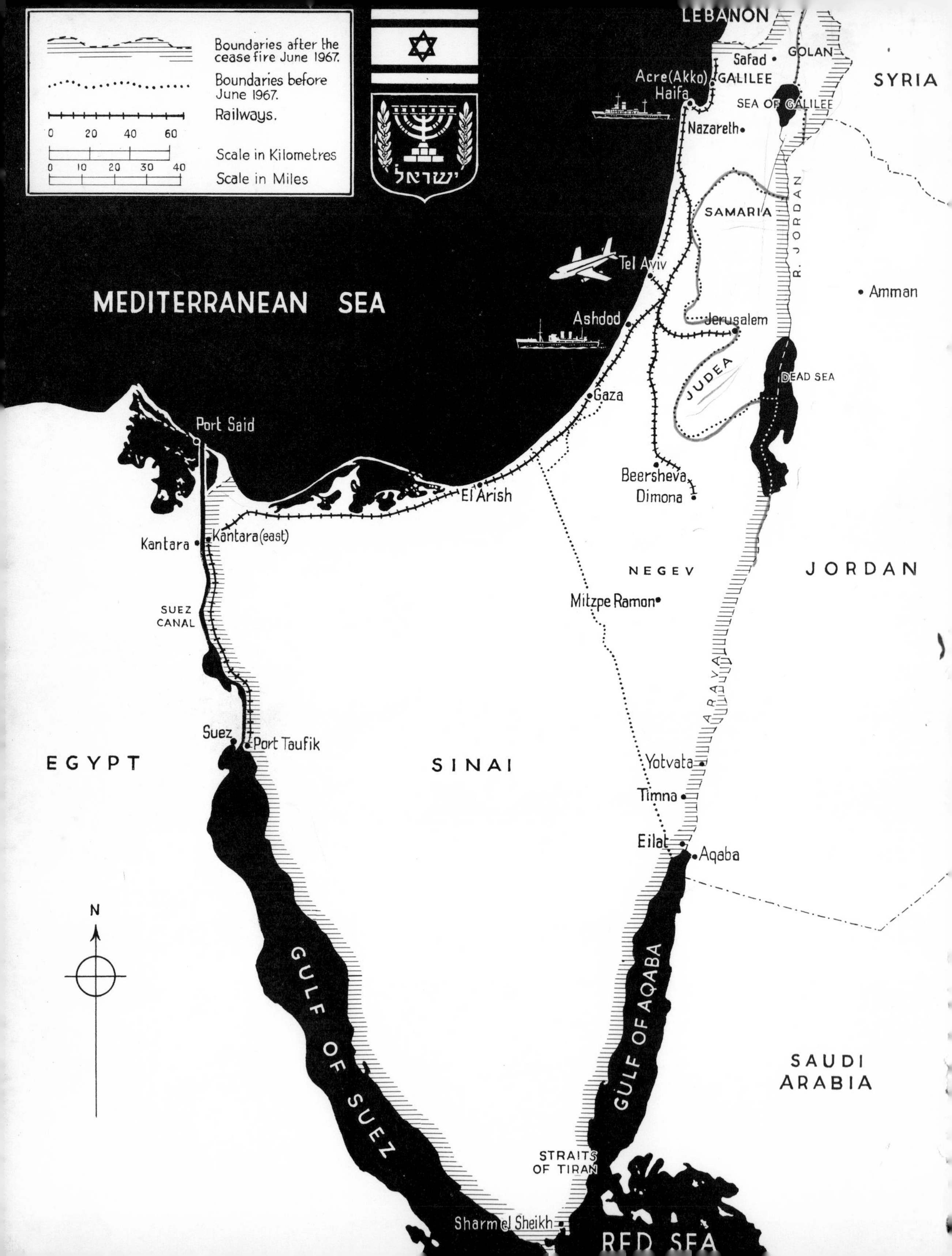
Boundaries after the cease fire June 1967.
Boundaries before June 1967.
Railways.
0 20 40 60
Scale in Kilometres
0 10 20 30 40
Scale in Miles
ישראל
LEBANON
GOLAN
Safad
SYRIA
Acre(Akko)
GALILEE
Haifa
SEA OF GALILEE
Nazareth
SAMARIA
R. JORDAN
Tel Aviv
Amman
MEDITERRANEAN SEA
Ashdod
Jerusalem
JUDEA
DEAD SEA
Gaza
Port Said
Beersheva
Dimona
El Arish
Kantara
Kantara(east)
NEGEV
JORDAN
Mitzpe Ramon
SUEZ
CANAL
ARAVA
Suez
Port Taufik
EGYPT
SINAI
Yotvata
Timna
Eilat
Aqaba
N
GULF OF SUEZ
GULF OF AQABA
SAUDI
ARABIA
STRAITS
OF TIRAN
Sharm el Sheikh
RED SEA